Convulsi
2021-4:
a Trusstercluck

Poems by
Chris Norris

Images by
Martin Gollan

"The major western democracies are moving towards corporatism. Democracy has become a business plan, with a bottom line for every human activity, every dream, every decency, every hope. The main parliamentary parties are now devoted to the same economic policies—socialism for the rich, capitalism for the poor—and the same foreign policy of servility to endless war. This is not democracy. It is to politics what McDonalds is to food."

—John Pilger

Text copyright © Chris Norris
Images © Martin Gollan
Edited by Mike Quille
Layout, typesetting & design by Alan Morrison
ISBN 978-1-912710-64-5

Acknowledgments

Many thanks for many reasons to David Blakesley, José Cifuentes, Freda Edis, Tim Evans, Rahim Hassan, Mike Jenkins, Torgeir Fjeld, Peter Thabit Jones, Wendy Lewis, Rebecca Lowe, Lucy Newlyn, and Rhoda Thomas.

My wife Valerie heard me out and helped me through; Mike Quille and Alan Morrison at Culture Matters did a marvellous job of editing and production; and Martin Gollan once again came up with some brilliantly pointed and suitably ferocious cartoons.

Greetings also to my comrades in Cor Cochion Caerdydd (the Cardiff Reds Choir) for decades of support, solidarity, and uplift jointly political and musical.

Contents

Introduction

By Chris Norris

These are political poems written between 2021 and 2024 in support of left-wing socialism and against the corrupt, divisive, racist, grossly inegalitarian, and often downright barbaric brand of Conservatism that the UK has witnessed, and suffered, for the past fourteen years.

We are now—as of January 2024—looking forward to a UK General Election later this year in which, as current polls indicate, the Tories should confront something between large-scale upset and near-total wipeout. Simply listing the names of a few of those involved—Rishi Sunak, Liz Truss, Kwasi Kwarteng, Priti Patel, Suella Braverman, Thérèse Coffey, Nadim Zahawi, Robert Jenrick, and James Cleverly, not to mention old hands in iniquity like David Cameron, John Redwood and Jacob Rees-Mogg—should conjure up memories of the period and the sheer squalid farce to which UK politics regularly sank in its brief but tempestuous course. I hope and trust the Tory party will soon be reduced to a tiny fringe of disreputable whingers representing the last hold-out zones of privilege, ignorance and greed.

This collection is intended in part as a reminder of how bad things were at that time and in part as a pre-emptive, I trust not premature, celebration of its close. Boris Johnson gets only the odd mention since ousted before the current (late-2023) lot took over though his lingering, malign and corrupting influence is everywhere felt in their words and actions. Keir Starmer gets a poem though more of a ticking-off for weaknesses and instances of policy backtracking which one hopes—albeit against all precedent—he'll reverse if and when elected.

Political poetry and song

As befits such a period the pieces vary in mode between savage indignation and melancholy reflection on present-day social ills, evils and injustices. They are all examples of formal verse, that is, poems with various kinds of rhyme-scheme, metre and stanza-form rather than 'free-verse' productions. The genres range from ballad, tanka and clerihew to quatrain, sonnet, and terza rima, with some—like 'The Enough's Enough Song'—written with an eye (or ear) to an existing, well-known tune.

It seems to me—after nearly four decades of street-singing with a socialist choir (Cor Cochion Caerdydd)—that political poetry had better stay in touch with political song if it is to make its point with maximum passion, conviction and communicative power. This case is one I've put to readers who criticised my earlier volumes of political verse on account of my using 'conservative' devices like rhyme and metre or 'archaic' forms like those mentioned above. Their objection stems from the presumptive affinity between radical poetics and radical politics, or between poetry committed to one or other of the schools, movements or factions that succeeded early C20 literary Modernism and, by dubious analogy, a politics avowedly well to the left of mainstream UK or US quasi-socialist alternatives.

I call it 'dubious' for three reasons. First, there is my point, as above, that political poems work best when they have a singing line. This is not to say that they must be meant for, or somehow lend themselves to, vocal-musical performance but rather that their impact is greatly increased by the expressive aspect of rhyme and the shifting interaction of metre with natural speech-rhythms.

Second, free verse is by very definition—in so far as it lives up to its name—distinctly lacking in just those qualities that put poetry most closely into contact with the living energies of emotionally charged, angry, sorrowful, urgently direct and above all powerfully collective speech.

Third, we have the preeminent examples of Brecht, Auden, Tony Harrison, Louis MacNeice, and Muriel Rukeyser—along with songwriter-poets like Woody Guthrie, Phil Ochs, Holly Near, Peggy Seeger, Leon Rosselson, and (intermittently) Bob Dylan—to show what these precepts amount to in creative practice. For they are all canny if unobtrusive formalists whose lyrics, however punchy and idiomatic, would have nothing like the same cogency without their keen ear for elements of form as well as force. At any rate these are the points I come back with when reproached for having lately abandoned, even betrayed, the post-structuralist commitments of my earlier writings as a literary theorist.

Political cartoons and satire

I also put the case that political poetry has much in common, technically as well as affectively speaking, with the way that political cartoons hit the mark if they succeed in changing people's attitudes, beliefs, or voting behaviour. The equivalent in a verse-satire or verse-polemic is when rhyme, metre and stanza-form combine to pick out the target like crosshairs in a rifle-sight, along with the sense that moral justice has been done without recourse to such drastic means.

Thus, the old, mostly cynical wisdom that says love and hate are close relatives does have its point as applied to poetry. Hate-poems, like love-poems, work best when they have the formal resources to express the kinds of passional intensity—negative or positive—that can't be conveyed by any other means. No doubt we should always blame the sin, not the sinner, but the verse-satirist again resembles the cartoonist in having only human material to work with.

Still there is a risk of satire becoming, as it does even in a master practitioner such as Jonathan Swift, an instrument so powerful and all-consuming that it threatens to pull down the very structures of thought and judgment in a paroxysm of rage. Martin Gollan's cartoons—here as in my previous Culture Matters collection—are exemplary in striking just the right balance of justified anger and formal as well as emotional control.

One danger this avoids is the kind of moral, social and political impotence that comes—as with certain initially hard-hitting TV panel shows—of cynicism constantly feeding off its own end-of-ideology wisecracks. Savage indignation is not the only mode in which satire operates so these poems include a fair sprinkling of humorous or better-tempered pieces in forms—like the clerihew or tanka—well-suited to that purpose.

Mockery, even gentle mockery, has its place in a political culture so largely given over to the brutal infliction of ruling-class interests and imperatives on a working class nowadays increasingly reduced to the condition of a market-dependent precariat. But when it comes to hitting them verbally where it hurts —the fossil-fuel lobbyists, oil-industry CEOs, arms-company executives, collusive politicians, corrupt journalists, or refugee-hating Government ministers —there is nothing like good old full-blooded Juvenalian satire.

The US-backed coup in Chile

One poem—the extended piece on Pablo Neruda—is here to offer a longer perspective on these topical themes and figures. What happened to Neruda, the great love poet and political activist, was the consequence of US (and therefore, to some extent, UK Government) machinations together with the active involvement of the arms industry and other corporate interests, most notoriously that of IBM. The 1973 military coup in Chile—headed by General Augusto Pinochet—led to the murder, torture, or disappearance of over thirty thousand leftists and others opposed to the regime.

It was a coup on behalf of neo-liberal capitalist ideologues whose doctrines are still the received wisdom amongst those who, calamitously, set the agenda for much of what passes as UK economic as well as social policy. After all, Pinochet was the welcome guest of Margaret Thatcher and her Chancellor Norman Lamont when he visited Britain and continued to enjoy their support when facing extradition to Spain on the charge of crimes against humanity. One may reasonably infer that Thatcher agreed with him as to the justification for mass murder when undertaken to protect the global reach of the neo-liberal economic order. Chile 1973 was a large part of my own, somewhat belated political awakening and remains so now as we enter the year of its fiftieth anniversary.

It is of course in the nature of a collection like this to be often overtaken by new and unignorable events when the deadline for submission looms uncomfortably close. As I write (January 2024) we are witnessing a genocidal Israeli military campaign to destroy Gaza and unleash yet another episode of mass civilian slaughter. It was already being called a humanitarian disaster 'of Biblical proportions' before the Israeli Prime Minister, Binyamin Netanyahu, all too knowingly literalised the usage by quoting Old Testament incitements to ethnic violence of just that totally indiscriminate and utterly barbaric nature.

My poem 'In Whose Bad Books?' addresses the issue of resurgent religious fundamentalism, not only in its Zionist but also in its US right-wing evangelical forms, each of them politically, morally and culturally the product of a massive regression in the currency of public discourse. As so often the UK has gone along with all this as an ally (= satellite or client state) of the US.

Just this morning (January 12th 2024) we woke to the news that Rishi Sunak had authorised the bombing of Houthi drone-missile launch-sites and other installations on account of their having attacked ships in the Red Sea that were carrying arms to assist in the Israeli genocide. This action was justified by the usual talk of free trade, economic interests, rights of passage, and rising commodity prices with scarcely a mention of the moral imperative to bring the atrocities to an end. Likewise as usual the BBC news services lent themselves to the propaganda war with minimal airtime found for opposing voices.

Morally impervious to the ongoing Palestinian slaughter—and seemingly ignorant of the Suez Canal precedent—Sunak has shown himself every inch the investment banker, as much in his domestic economic policies as his choice of wider political alignments. My poems about him were written at moments of maximum disgust with everything he stands for and I very much hope that this comes across undiluted by any passage of time.

Collusion in genocide

The US and UK collusion with Israel—especially in the supply of huge amounts of weaponry—amounts to very active collusion in genocide and is, quite simply, unforgivable. Another piece, 'Pretexts: Amalek', takes aim at Netanyahu's use of a particularly blood-curdling Old Testament passage to authorise, justify and further incite the ongoing crimes against humanity. What is taking shape under these joint US and UK government auspices is something like a full-scale, massively armed and corporately-backed crusading version of the Christian-Zionist fringe sects that have for some time been peddling their various strains of Apocalypse Now (or Very Soon). Great material for the satirist and activist but terrible in what it says about the present-day state of UK, US and global politics.

Oddly enough, if there's one episode that offers hope of an end to this whole wretched tale then it is the farcically brief spell (49 days) during which Liz Truss was British Prime Minister. What she and her Chancellor of the Exchequer, Kwasi Kwarteng, managed to do was to push Tory economic doctrines so recklessly and absurdly far that the consequences were plain to see—economic disaster—and 'the markets' decided the experiment must end.

Maybe it's wishful thinking to interpret that rebuff to the far-right think-tanks, IMF wonks and Sunak-clones as presaging the collapse of neo-liberal orthodoxy, along with its ideological figleaf, the 'trickle-down' theory of wealth distribution. But that's very much what it felt like at the time and subsequent developments on the economic front have done nothing to disconfirm initial—optimistic—impressions. The closing verse-letter to Jeremy Corbyn will I think give a pretty good idea of which way my current hopes and sympathies run.

Swansea
January 2024

On the Tory Leadership Hustings, September 2022

A hundred-and-fifty thousand votes
Those Party members cast.
A hundred-and-fifty thousand votes,
That's all it took to burn our boats,
To have the bailiffs at our throats—
Gas-meters ticking fast, you know,
Those meters ticking fast.

We saw them sitting row on row,
The Tory rank-and-file.
We saw them sitting row on row,
The party faithful—same old show
Of ugly mugs with loads of dough,
All oozing hate and bile, you know,
Just oozing hate and bile.

By sixty, people have a face
That gives out all the signs.
By sixty, it's a striking case
Of sold-as-seen, and what a place
This freak-show is for those who'd trace
The rich-folk's worry-lines, you know,
Those rich-folk's worry-lines.

They worry that the plebs might take
A quick look down their way.
They worry lest those losers stake
Their squatters' chance at make-or-break,
And say, 'it's for the kiddies' sake',
Since 'that's what their sort say, you know,
The kind of thing they say'.

They worry that 'those union thugs'
Might get the folk onside,
Not turn out one more bunch of mugs

But earn the people's cheers and hugs
By pulling all the bankers' plugs
To end their long free ride, you know,
Their decades-long free ride.

But most of all it's that word 'strike'
That spooks those conferees.
Their faces say 'no wages-hike
For you lot, just get on your bike,
Or starve, whichever way you like'
They want you on your knees, you know,
Want you lot on your knees.

I watched them as they snarled and smirked,
I watched them as they girned,
And thought: well, plainly something's worked,
Some ghastly dream has got them irked
(As one old snorer twitched and jerked),
And that's a lesson learned, you know,
A useful lesson learned.

It tells us: brightest day may dawn
After the darkest night.
Those faces wreathed in hatred, scorn,
Derision, fear, like gargoyles born
Of haunted sleep, may, come the morn,
Be bathed in purest light, who knows?,
Fresh-bathed in purest light.

But keep it well in mind, that scene,
Like Goya's glimpse of hell,
Projected on the TV screen
With all the avarice and spleen
That drives the Tory hate-machine
To cast its evil spell, you know,
That evil Tory spell.

We'll beat the thing, the hideous thing,
The Tory scourge we dread.
We'll march, we'll shout, we'll talk, we'll sing,
We'll agitate, join forces, spring
Surprise invasions, all to bring
The crisis to a head, you know,
This crisis to a head.

For there's no antidote so strong
As what's on offer there.
See how they flock, that aging throng,
To those who'll do the gravest wrong,
And how they answer like a gong
When hate-talk fills the air, you know,
When hate-talk fills the air.

Let's up and rid ourselves of those
Old tools of grift and greed.
Let's spur the outrage as it grows,
Distinguish clearly: friends and foes,
Make sure it's ours, the way it goes,
And stuff their Tory creed, you know,
Just stuff their Tory creed!

Love and Politics: a tanka

(Japanese extended haiku-like verse form: 31 syllables in all; lines of 5, 7, 5, 7, 7 syllables, rhyming ababb)

1 (Love Poet)

Love is life sublime!
So say we lovers, crooners,
We who'd spend our time
Banging dustbin-lids soon as
Strike up with you harsh tuners!

Give us the sweet stuff,
Love-songs, poems lyrical,
Not rough-house street stuff
Or verses satirical—
Why scant it, love's miracle?

For god's sake spare us
That Brechtian sermonising;
Don't try to scare us
By constantly devising
Plans for the next uprising.

Just leave us piping
Those love-songs, lyrics graceful
Like ours, not sniping
Or letting fly a case-full
Of slogans in-your-face-ful.

So here's a handy
Tip from us: do please treasure
The love-struck dandy
Whose every lyric measure
Brings value-added pleasure.

2 (Activist Poet)

Croon on, you luvvies!
Carry on cuddling, kissing;
'Push-come-to-shove' is
The one item missing
From all your commie-dissing.

You lyric poets,
Spare us your love-clamouring—
Surely you know it's
The bother-boots hammering
That message: 'quit yammering!'.

Sure, better tucked up
In bed with your darling-hearts,
Not getting sucked up
In it when the snarling starts,
Or batons on body-parts.

Just spare us a thought,
Us anti-racist fighters,
When we're up in court
And those race-hate inciters
Go free, like lyric-writers!

See how we're taking
The flak while you continue
With your love-making,
And how only our sinew
Holds back the thug who'd chin you.

So, love-bird, let it
Sink in: you're perching
On Cloud Nine, get it?,
And all your deep soul-searching
Won't stop the branches lurching!

Boss-talk: Sunak

Let's screw those losers, show them who's the boss!
We're screwed already, no pips left to squeak.
They'll never twig: our profit means their loss:
Let's screw those losers, show them who's the boss!
We've twigged: we're screwed and you don't give a toss.
Must have been some sacked underling's last leak,
Some mate you've shafted, keen to put across
What trash you are (suspects not far to seek!).
Let's screw those losers, show them who's the boss!
We're screwed already, no pips left to squeak.

Best way to fool them: say we're cutting tax!
Ah, that old trick—you pulled it way back when.
We'll say we've got, not that we're on, their backs!
Best way to fool them: say we're cutting tax!
A bit of savvy's what that game-plan lacks.
We swallowed it before, but that was then,
And now we know: the rich will get the max
Relief while we get chicken-feed again.
Best way to fool them: say we're cutting tax!
Ah, that old trick—you pulled it way back when.

No problem—lots of new tricks in my bag!
All trashy stuff, catchpenny voter-bribes.
If that fails we'll just wave the Union Flag,
No problem—lots of new tricks in my bag!
Check 'Rishi Sunak, barrel-scrape, hashtag'.
A fraudster's pitch—gives off all the wrong vibes;
Smart shirt and tie but sounds like an old lag.
Already I can hear the backbench jibes.
No problem—lots of new tricks in my bag!
All trashy stuff, catchpenny voter-bribes.

Don't worry, chums, we'll get the poor to pay!
Don't bet on it, investment-banker trash.
We'll starve you out or find some other way:
Don't worry, chums, we'll get the poor to pay!
We've got your number, spurn us as you may:
For all your posh mates, private jets, and cash
To spare you'll find out, post-election day,
That it's all gone in one almighty crash.
Don't worry, chums, we'll get the poor to pay.
Don't bet on it, investment-banker trash.

I'll crush your hovels with my Gucci shoes.
We'll give you hell for leather, rich-kid Rish!
Starve, beg, sleep under bridges—yours to choose:
I'll crush your hovels with my Gucci shoes.
We've all to gain, you've everything to lose.
Banged up in gaol you won't look quite so swish
When needless deaths from Covid hit the news
And 'eat out, help out' proves a poison dish.
I'll crush your hovels with my Gucci shoes.
We'll give you hell for leather, rich-kid Rish!

I tell you, plebs: time's up for folk like you.
We tell you, Rish: the writing's on the wall!
I'm here to fight for us, the wealthy few,
And tell you, plebs: no time for folk like you.
The time must come when justice claims its due,
When sleazy, bent prime ministers must fall,
And it's our turn at last to twist the screw
(Of justice, this time!) on your vile cabal.
I tell you, plebs: no time for folk like you.
We tell you, Rish: the writing's on the wall!

To the Lukewarm

So, because you are lukewarm, and neither hot nor cold, I will spit you out of my mouth.

—Revelation 3:16

Let hate, like love, burn steady, fierce and clean.
No time for cooling passions—keep your flame
Turned up, spot-on: oxyacetylene!

Try this: the man has lied, shifted the blame
To hapless functionaries, fled the scene
Of every crime before some reckoner came

To call him out, obstructed justice, been
Lead player in each tabloid-sponsored game
Of rabble-rousing, skulked behind a screen

Of bluff and bluster when a one-time tame
Investigator spilled the final bean
On some new crime-in office, staked his claim

To rank with Nero in the epicene
Dictator league, got press-hounds to defame
A judge or two, rejoiced to vent his spleen

On those reporters rash enough to name
A host of scattered offspring or umpteen
Past mistresses, let slip that his chief aim

Was scrapping any pesky law they'd frame
To oust him, have the Met latch on he's keen
To hush their findings up, revealed that shame

Or honour have no place in the latrine
Of quick-flush conscience, and displayed the same
Old Eton-bred contempt that's let them preen

Themselves, those would-be monarchs, on their fame
For all things bad, like this one and his queen
Whose sins, Macbeth-like, darken each *je t'aime.*

To the Frogs: a message (sent AD 2050)

It's thirty years ago today,
Full thirty years ago,
They put us 'criminals' away
In case we stole the show.

They said: 'don't let those stop-the-oil
Protesters get off free
So they can do their best to spoil
Your True Brit liberty.

Let little kids breathe noxious air,
Keep diesels sputtering on,
And show the vandals you don't care—
Let ULEZ zones be gone!'.

The politicians played along
For fear the red-wall voters
Would soon revolt at actions strong
Enough to hit their motors.

Then there were fossil-fuel lobbyists,
Oil company CEOs,
And ministers whose grubby fists
Were stuffed with quid pro quos.

Those monsters didn't give a toss
If kids grew sick or died
So long as profits made their loss
A fact to brush aside.

The PM was a nowhere-man,
A cut-out of a suit,
His morals even viler than
His hedge-fund garnered loot.

And so it went from week to week
And stifling year to year
Till we'd gone far up Doomsday Creek
And the end-times drew near.

But then we thought: what fools we've been
To let them rule the roost
And make last-act Anthropocene
A shit-show they've produced.

Let's take the fight to them, let's try
To put the fear of god
Into all those who'll see us fry
To get the markets' nod.

It's clear we've left it far too late
To turn this thing around
While they, the few, decreed our fate:
A world destruction-bound.

They lied, they schemed, they fixed the press,
They did the Doomsday sums
And figured: few years more or less—
Let's take it as it comes!

The PM thought 'not hard to fool
The plebs—just see you get
The press onside with private pool
And jaunts by private jet'.

And so it went, yet no-one thought
To call the boss-class bluff,
To voice the only plain retort:
'You swine, we've had enough.

It's time we need, the time to win
It back, the time we've lost,
Or some part of it, and begin
At last to count the cost.

Then we can reckon what it takes
To cleanse the public sphere
Of those for whom it's private stakes
Alone that they hold dear'.

That's what we thought, and said, and made
The key-point of our call
For folk at last to grasp what they'd
Brought on us, that cabal.

The crisis hit, it brought despair,
Grief, suffering on a scale
Beyond the power of words to share
Once words of warning fail.

But we'd brought some folk to accept
It's bad when private wealth
And interests of state aren't kept
Apart but linked by stealth.

We'd shown them: it's your kids, grandkids,
And all the multitude
Of future lives on whom the lid's
Now being tightly screwed.

And so the tables swiftly turned
As people saw the crime
For what it was at last, and learned
How best to buy more time.

Oh yes, the judge and jury deemed
Us few the guilty men,
Yet please think: what if we'd not teamed
Up rapidly back then?

Let no-one say we took the law
Into our own bad hands,
When what we dissidents first saw
The world now understands.

Those climate-change deniers strove
To bring extinction forward
As forest fires torched every grove
And panicked crowds fled shoreward.

Fossil-fuel lobbyists would tell
Whatever lies might do
To push us lemmings to the hell
Whose portents they well knew.

I say the fear of god we struck
Into their guilty souls
Was what enabled hope to pluck
A spark from smouldering coals.

We paid the price for you who still
Have time enough to start
Out bravely on the long uphill
Post-cataclysmic part.

But don't be caught with your guard down,
Don't let them loose, those men
Dead-set to batter, boil or drown
All creature-kind again.

And don't wake up to find you've played
The sucker's role once more
And, like a slow-boiled frog, obeyed
The life-destroyer's law.

Another Vote for Sunak!

Me, I'm your typical swing voter—
The only thing I care about's my car.
Just keep your hands off me and my old motor
Else you'll find out how narky us lot are.

That Sunak, he won't screw my daily rota.
He knows this barmy Ulez thing's by far
The biggest issue for your cash-strapped floater—
It's all them doomsday types whose voices jar!

If I was Rishi's party-line promoter
I'd say 'just get old Clarkson as your czar
For drivers' rights— he'd push the Ulez boat a
Whole lot farther out, our all-time star!

So tell the world we don't care one iota
How anxious for their grandkids' lungs they are,
Those Greens—we say 'Jump back in your Toyota
And we'll jump back in our old bangers, ta!'

Pretexts: Amalek

Benjamin Netanyahu twice 'invoked the Biblical story of the total destruction of Amalek', declaring 'You must remember what Amalek has done to you, says our Holy Bible. And we do remember'. A later passage in the Bible leaves no doubt for interpretation: 'Now go and smite Amalek, and utterly destroy all that they have, and spare them not; but slay both man and woman, infant and suckling, ox and sheep, camel and ass'. This was no throwaway comment.

—Owen Jones, *The Guardian*, 13th January 2024

Open your holy book and I'll show you,
Before too long, some passage fit to scare
The toughest thug or battle-hardened guy.

There's things in it you always sort-of knew
From church or Sunday School but couldn't square
With 'God is love', so chose to overfly.

You go to church and, in a nearby pew,
A kindly woman kneels in silent prayer,
Then stands, goes forward, and calls to God on high

For His too-tardy vengeance on some crew
Of heathens who've been singled out to bear,
As if by blood-crazed monster in the sky,

The kind of tribal savagery that drew
God-squads of every creed to grab their share
Of neighbour-goods with scripture's alibi.

Does she, the lesson-reader, have a clue
What this stuff's all about, how they prepare,
Those passages, for demagogues who'll try,

In evil times, their God-backed best to do
Just what Saul did and bid the victors spare
No man, woman or child. *Let them all die,*

The curst Amalekites, lest God eschew
The Covenant with His people and declare
Himself henceforth deaf to their every cry.

Think of them afterwards, those foes you slew,
As swine fit only to pollute the air
Breathed by our prophets whom their gods defy!

Then you, His chosen people, will stay true
To the one God and vanquish all who dare
Thus spurn the laws and customs you live by.

Thus spake the frauds and zealots who well knew
How best to rouse the xenophobes with their
High dictates set in stone on Mount Sinai.

It's now and in our time the call's come through
Once more, the shouts, the screams, the trumpet's blare,
And, far beyond the endless eye-for-eye

Of custom's law, the hideous *déjà vu*
Of Biblical atrocities that bear
The mark of having yet to satisfy

The cravings of a God whose rightful due
Includes the genocidal *droit de guerre*
That holy book and prophets' words supply.

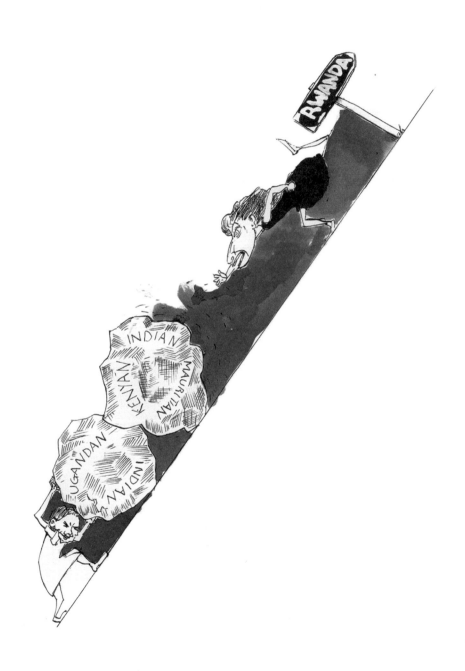

Of Wickedness and Evil in a Tory Sense

Suella Braverman has a 'dream'. And what is it that she dreams of? Yesterday, she let an audience at a Conservative conference fringe event in on one of her great political hopes: a *Telegraph* front page with a picture of a plane taking off to Rwanda. This, her big dream, is the stuff of many people's nightmares.

Later the same day, in her first major speech as Home Secretary, Braverman thanked Priti Patel for the 'foundations' she had laid in toughening the immigration system, invoking the usual spectres of 'illegal immigrants', 'low-skilled foreign workers' and 'mass and rapid migration'. But she made it clear that she would go further, with plans to bring in the harshest, most damaging immigration environment yet.

—Maya Goodfellow, *The Guardian*, 5th October 2022

You think there is no difference, but you're wrong!
It's what the worst kind trade on, that you'll fail
Or not attempt to tell it, so that they'll
Have you on board and sure to go along
With monstrous policies however strong
The stench of evil or the massive scale
Of human suffering it may entail
As their fore-reckoned consequences throng
To bring the difference home. I'm speaking here
Of wickedness and evil, often used
As if they might be switched with no great loss
Of moral purchase, or with no great fear
That this might leave us hopelessly confused
With cases that we daily come across.

The Graham Greene thing (Pinkie, *Brighton Rock*):
You're meant to feel there's something off-the-scale
About that teenage killer, something they'll
Not get their heads around, the docile flock
Of good-to-bad types whom his actions shock
And horrify, from the first death (poor Hale!)
To Rose's grief, yet who'll forever fail

To grasp how putting Pinkie in the dock
Was somehow off the point. OK, that's Greene,
You'll tell me, that shrewd loader of the dice
Who'll slip the Catholic message in to say
'Reader, you err: there's mercy shown between
The stirrup and the ground; grace may suffice
For ends no pious moral can convey'.

Indeed, we're being got at, and we'd best
Resist the plot-mechanics and the way
They're rigged to place some kind of weird cachet
On Pinkie's standing out above the rest
For top score in the touch-of-evil test
And thereby showing how the *dieu caché*
Of Greene's perverse creation has us play
Our role with blowzy Ida in the quest
For merely mortal justice. Just compare
That odd remark of Eliot (T. S.)
About the safely damned who walk secure
In their damnation, such as Baudelaire,
Out sauntering the boulevards and less
Hell-bothered now he deems the prospect sure.

A kind of snobbery, this ploy to get
A quick god-levered one-up on all those
Well-meaning, liberal-minded types who'll close
The novel and discover they've been set
Down firmly, if with Greene's sincere regret,
On the wrong side since at some point they chose,
Like Ida, to ignore God only knows
What occult signs or clues might else have let
Them in on His intent. So much for how
It works in fictive mode, this non-unique
(Think Muriel Spark!) yet strange desire to draw
An extra sheep/goat line that might allow
Those so inclined to treat it, that mystique,
As joint divine-and-novelistic law.

But turn from fiction to the messier sphere
Of politics and you'll most likely find
A need for that distinction you declined
When put to work in crafty ways to steer
Us down Cathedral Close. A rare thing here,
That touch of evil, but keep it in mind
When next some politician of the kind
'Tory Home Secretary' bends your ear
With racist taunts We've had two such in three
Years now, both women, both the kind who hate
Themselves as much as those they so despise
Since the words 'immigrant', or 'refugee',
Or—worst—'asylum-seeker' names a state
Their parents faced and they must exorcise.

Amongst their colleagues wickedness is more
The norm, not evil, though you might well think
The difference is one you'd rather sink
Than try to make stick every time that you're
Confronted with some instance you deplore
And 'wicked' trembles briefly on the brink
Of that far stronger term from which you shrink
Since over-use will soon deplete its store
Of moral obloquy. Still just as well
To get the difference straight: it's the true mark
Of evil that, like Milton's Satan, faced
With cosmos-wide division (let's leave hell
And Greene-land out of it) the choice is stark:
'Evil, be thou my good', calmly embraced.

Of wicked types you'll find no shortage should
You future scanners of the present scene
In UK politics contain your spleen
For long enough to see just how things stood
With us so far as reckoned on the good-
V-bad (or wicked) scale where there's no clean,
Decisive break-point as there is between

The evil-doer and the neighbourhood
Of mundane vice and virtue. No denying
It's bad, the short-of-evil wicked stuff,
The graft, corruption, cash-for-questions, sleaze,
Backhanders, sweeteners, bribes, collusion, lying,
And favours done for gifts received enough
To fill a county gaol with bent MPs.

What's come of it, you'll ask, that line I'm so
Resolved to draw, that litmus-test for what's
Plain evil and what moral sense allots
To the mid-range where cases mostly go
From good to wicked. Here you'll turn up no
Home Secretaries who'll tie themselves in knots
Of moral self-abasement to find spots
In some far place or vile regime to stow
Their hated alter egos. It's that twist,
That loathing born of every baulked desire
For pure belonging, native or divine,
That drives the migrant-hater to resist
The last faint conscience-call should it conspire
With all that complicates their story-line.

And yet that photo says: 'please know that I've
No willed or willing part in it, that there's
Some force that seizes me, all unawares,
And has me turn them back when they arrive
Exhausted on our shores, those just-alive
Asylum-seekers whom the Channel spares
From drowning only for the brusque 'who cares?'
Of one whose parents chanced to stay and thrive,
Unlike those hapless souls'. Not off the hook
By this, morally speaking, but contrast
The way those features harden in the grip
Of near-demonic hatred with the look
Of furtive wickedness that might just last
A moment when some routine lie's let slip.

You'll say 'We're back to Greene or Orson Welles,
Back in some spooky precinct, what with all
This touch-of-evil stuff they hold on call
For conjuring up the kind of frisson hell's
Still good for on occasion, though the spell's
Not one that works so well with a cabal
Of squalid politicians who'd each fall
More aptly on a moral scale that tells
Simply how bad they are'. And I'd assent:
Greene-land's a place where morals turn perverse,
Where being damned becomes a glamour-stock,
Where speech-acts kill no matter how well-meant,
And lives go on beneath some primal curse
That says good thoughts return only to mock.

This much agreed, still there's the benefit
(If that's the word) of seeing how the signs
Of evil grow, how hatred self-refines
From childhood fears, and how the Native-Brit
Desire in those who doubt they're quite legit
May breed a monster fit to meet the lines
Of refugees sharp-clawed as it repines
At the mere thought of that asylum chit
They'd stamped 'Mixed Asian-Kenyan'. Best you keep
A sense of it, the difference that consists
Not in some notion of those souls elect
Since well and truly damned but in the deep
And stigma-nurtured malice that enlists
A covert cheer for every boat-load wrecked.

For strip that old word 'evil' of the vibes
It's picked up over centuries of use
By bible-bashers keen to reproduce
God-sanctioned feuds between the rival tribes
Of true believers and you'll see the scribes
Reveal, unwittingly, what's now let loose
By politicians seeking some excuse

To up the racist rhetoric from jibes
To verbal limpet-mines. Don't be deceived:
There's evil stirring every time that spite
Turns visceral and takes its chance to seize
On fears, resentments, ancient hurts retrieved,
And psyches twisted to detach the plight
Of past from all-too-present refugees.

The Good Old Cause Revived: a Ballad

It is also affirm'd from diligent search made in our ancient books of Law, that the
Peers and Barons of England had a legal right to judge the King: which was the
cause most likely, for it could be no slight cause, that they were call'd his Peers,
or equals. This however may stand immovable, so long as man hath to deal with
no better than man; that if our Law judge all men to the lowest by their Peers, it
should in all equity ascend also, and judge the highest.

—John Milton, *The Tenure of Kings and Magistrates* (1649)

I tell you, Sirs: they'll bless the day
This new pretender died,
Although I know the price I'll pay—
A signed-up regicide!

Let fortune treat me as it may
Should ill events betide,
Crowned heads regain their ancient sway,
And freedom be denied.

It's Milton's role, the one I'll play,
That poet who supplied
An epic fit to join the fray
With Satan as our guide!

Read it aright and see him stray
From all that's certified
As holy writ and have us weigh
The devil's case clear-eyed.

Then you'll, like me, elect to lay
Old pieties aside,
Think God the devil, and hurray
The rebels in their pride!

It's sovereign power they'd keep at bay,
Demand what's bona fide
About God's role as prop and stay
Of kings with much to hide.

Why keep the wastrels making hay,
Why grant them that free ride,
When there's a quick and ready way
That's all too seldom tried?

I say it's not a man they slay,
Those few who can't abide
The servile thought of mortal clay
By mortal souls enskied.

Divine Right! that's the doctrine they
Revile, and one that I'd
Kill in him sooner than betray
The virtuous path we've plied.

For there's no king can say us nay,
No future Charles to chide
Us free-born souls who'll not obey
What vassals take in stride.

There's times to come when folk will say
'It's they who stopped the slide;
Else we'd have Charleses to this day,
As Milton prophesied'.

Night Thoughts of a Home Secretary

They ask me constantly, as if I care!
They say: 'why persecute those refugees?
God knows they've had hard times enough to bear!
Why turn a stone-deaf ear to all their pleas?'
I tell them: 'we've got refugees to spare
And anyway, they reckon it's a breeze,
Those fake asylum seekers, touting their
Heart-wrenching life-events, their histories
Of war, expulsion, fire-storms from the air,
Death-dealing armies, boat-capsizing seas,
And all the stuff they think will set them fair
For UK residence, hand them the keys
To what they deem their god-appointed share
Of Britishness—no go, you deportees!'.

And then they say: 'how can you sleep at night,
How square it with your conscience, how ignore
The sheer hypocrisy that thinks it right
To send them back, those fugitives from war
And every kind of suffering, on a flight
To some place where they'll have to face yet more
Such griefs and terrors—and all this despite
The UK having shown an open door
To them, your parents, when the modern blight
Of 'ethnic cleansing' or the crescent roar
Of civil strife consigned them to the plight
You'd now inflict on those who reach our shore
And find a monster crouched to extradite
Them back to the same hell they'd known before'.

O snowflakes, your reproaches fall on ears
Long closed to such humanitarian cries!
That's why I warn they're swarming our frontiers,
Those economic migrants in the guise
Of refugees; and why, when they're deemed peers

29

Of mine, I then repudiate all ties
With them, all sense of common hopes and fears,
And hate them more for thinking they could rise
As high as me with my great twin careers
In Law and Politics, then—greatest prize
Of all—the office of Home Secretary where years
Of graft paid off and let me mobilize
The press to show those washers-up that here's
No place for them, no chance to advertise
Their paltry gifts and access all the spheres
Of influence a lawless lawyer buys.

Ballad of a Violent Man

That judge, he said the only way
With violent men like me
Is bang them up in gaol and say
We've thrown away the key.

He said I'd soon regret the day
I shook the Cyprus tree
And made my list of who should pay
The fitting penalty.

'Violent', he said, but who's to lay
That charge who cannot see
The monstrous kinds of violence they
Do daily yet go free?

'Address the jury, let them weigh
Your wicked words', said he,
'So they'll not let such notions sway
The upright citizenry'.

I took my chance and made my play,
Not just for sympathy
But in the hope that my words may
Outlive my 'guilty' plea.

For it's no shorter term I pray
He'll see fit to decree;
I wrote my list and knew I'd stay
Locked up long as could be.

Just think, I said, what violence they'd
Committed, those whom I
Myself judged fittest to be made,
Each one, a chief fall-guy.

First up, those knights of the arms-trade
Who thought 'Yeah, sure they'll die,
The women and kids, but I'm afraid
Not mine to reason why'.

Next up: the shameless suit-parade
Of bankers living high
On billions cunningly conveyed
Offshore as paupers die.

And next: the types who found it paid,
And handsomely, to buy
Up mortgages deemed bottom-grade
Then squeeze the homeless dry.

Then politicians, those who preyed
On folk who dared not try
The remedies class-law forbade
Lest risings multiply.

Let's not forget the press-brigade
Whose every sponsored lie
Subdued the cry for present aid
With pie in some far sky.

You speak of violence? Just compare
What the worst-off endure
For want of their entitled share
In a life-saving cure.

Think, too, of what those parents bear
Who have to reassure
Their starving kids it's waiting there,
The current *plat du jour*.

Consider then the billionaire
Whose hedge-fund stocks mature
Just as the bailiff knocks to scare
Those kids: wolf at the door!

I ask you city gents: how dare
You blame the sick and poor
For thoughts of violence when it's their
Bleak lives keep yours secure.

There's violence of the kind that hits
The headlines—guaranteed
To get the papers screaming 'it's
Tough gaol-regimes we need!'.

Then there's a whipped-up media blitz
As frothing hacks stampede
To find a gory tale that fits
The baying tabloid screed.

It's why I call them hypocrites
Who claim the moral lead
By making sure the vital bits
Are what no readers read.

Else they'd soon realise who commits
The crime when thousands bleed
And learn it's not the loner, it's
The system they should heed.

The system has a special slot
For each of them, those swine
Who hone whatever skills they've got
In the mass-murder line.

They kill not by the single shot
Or lone campaign like mine,
Or through some scarcely 'secret' plot
Of traceable design.

No, you'll not catch them out, that lot,
By tapping their grape-vine,
Or when you merely chance to spot
The message: 'coast clear—fine!'.

It's not like that they operate,
The profiteers of war,
The stirrers-up of ethnic hate,
And grinders of the poor.

Their system strikes like blows of fate,
It conjures shock and awe,
And tells us: 'not your business, mate!',
Just so we know the score.

They say 'Please see our balance-slate,
Wiped clean by CoverUp Corps,
And should some lawyer take the bait
Then we'll just change the law'.

They say 'You fools look to the State
For justice but ignore
The trade-rules we smart guys dictate
Through that revolving door'.

'So Parliament's set to debate
Those kids killed by the score?
Don't get your hopes up yet—just wait
Till our guy takes the floor!'.

They're beating us, I tell you straight,
Giving us the old what for,
So long as we prevaricate
And act as their cat's paw.

Their violence stalks the world, it kills
By cluster-bomb, by drone,
By sharply increased household bills,
And life-hopes swiftly blown.

It twists the honest worker's skills
To interests not his own,
Like a new hand-grenade that spills
More blood and splintered bone.

Be sure: it's by their corporate wills
Old folk must die alone,
And young folk too when violence fills
What living-space they've known.

Just feel how the cash-nexus chills
Each act of kindness shown,
Counts trust a fool's resort, and stills
Affection's vibrant tone.

Think hard, then name the human ills
That don't spring from the zone
Where capital perfects its drills
For draining blood from stone.

In Wall Street, Bourse, and Beverly Hills
The killer-blight has grown
And turned Blake's dark satanic mills
To death by pay-day loan.

So, when they talk of violence, let
My case not go for naught,
But tell the victims 'Don't forget
The bitter truths he taught'.

They'll flinch from it, they'll feel the threat
Of justice dearly bought,
And label you a friend ill-met
If they end up in court.

Yet there'll be some who won't regret
The change in them I wrought
By having crimes of state offset
My deeds of last resort.

The papers say 'he'll pay his debt'
And gleefully report
Each judge-recorded epithet
While skipping my retort.

But my few words will break through yet
And cut their message short,
Those tabloid hacks whose lies abet
Great crimes of every sort.

The folk will get to realise
How gross the shift of scale
As global death-tolls daily rise
While we lot go to gaol.

It's rules the fat cats legalize
That stop us getting bail,
Like that which says: they'll organize
If our laws don't prevail.

And every minute someone dies
To boost a new arms-sale,
And no-one hits those boss-class guys
We should be out to nail.

The debt-load figure multiplies,
Third-world economies fail,
And temperatures hit record highs
As oil-men blast the shale.

Jet-borne tycoons criss-cross the skies,
No missile on their tail,
As, down below, a mother tries
To quiet a starveling's wail.

No end to the new trading-ties
Those ministers unveil
As some new weaponry supplies
The stuff to blaze their trail.

How easily they make the switch,
From government to board
Of any firm that makes them rich—
Patience its own reward!

The thing goes through without a hitch
Since tactfully ignored
By the press-barons with an itch
To gain the title 'Lord'.

Ask the arms-buyer which is which
And he'll be truly floored:
'Same blokes, same sweeteners, same old pitch—
And same old whiff of fraud'.

They'd kill their grandmothers to stitch
Some rival up or hoard
Some extra cash so they can snitch
On friends they can't afford.

No violence greater than the kind
That comes in tailored suits,
Speaks posh, but begs we keep in mind
Their rise from humble roots.

They're all in it, their lives entwined,
All killers in cahoots,
Whose victims—i.d. unassigned—
No reckoner computes.

No messages they leave behind,
Those whom the system mutes,
No scrap of evidence to find
That tells who's killed, who shoots.

Else they say 'death: cause undefined'
And settle all disputes
Simply by keeping pockets lined
And paying off the brutes.

But justice knows it's flying blind
Each time its long pursuits
Meet wealth and wickedness combined
To pick up fresh recruits.

Still every system has its nodes,
Its points where two lines meet,
And maps are where the lines are roads,
And cross-roads mean club-feet,

And clubs are where the boss off-loads
His latest plan to beat
Some rival's smart computer codes
Or chase him off the street.

But it's not every bomb explodes
Where cross-marked on the sheet
That names us folk whose known abodes
He'd wish to feel the heat.

Take courage, friends: my soul forebodes
A system in retreat
If we repay the violence owed
By methods less discreet.

It's violence on that scale that goads
Your craving to defeat
The web of evil that erodes
Your soul: justice is sweet!

[Notes: the Cyprus tree is the tree of death in Greek mythology; cross-roads and club-feet are linked in Sophocles' *Oedipus*.]

A Plaint: to Keir Starmer

You're a bit of a dud, Mr Starmer,
And you're letting us down, I fear.
No, we're not looking out for a charmer,
Or a fun guy to tickle our ear,
Or a home-grown Barack Obama,
Or a BoJo to bring us fake cheer.
No, we'll happily skip the high drama
With you as a cut-price King Lear
If you'll just dump the old psychic armour,
Set the pace and not bring up the rear.
Else you'll find it's the wrong sort of karma,
Not Hardie's, that dubbed you 'Sir Keir'.

An Epistle to Mr Rishi Sunak

1

They don't come monster-like today,
Not as they came of old,
When Tories roused to toothsome prey
Like wolves amongst the fold.

No gross Dickensian mugs have they,
No manners icy-cold,
No sneering, leering, jeering way
Of telling us: Be told!

We almost miss them, almost say
'Alas, who's smashed the mould
That made their bestial display
A wonder to behold?'.

Of course they're still around, the stray
Survivors yet unsold
On sounding civilised since, hey,
We're Tories—big, bad, bold!

Still there's a quiet communiqué
Gone out to say 'we've polled
The hoi polloi so better stay
In line, play good as gold!

2

But don't be fooled: this latest lot
May smooth-talk, come across
As civil types, but still they've got
Your number: pleb, not boss!

Try striking, give it your best shot,
Turn profit into loss
For shareholders, and soon they'll spot
Some old class-law to gloss.

Else they'll just make new law and swat
Your rightful claim like dross
Best swept aside to show law's not
A stone that gathers moss.

Be warned: these types don't care a jot
Who's starving, forced to doss
Down in extremes of cold or hot:
Goose, gander—grab the sauce!

3

They come like city slickers, dressed
To play the markets, start
A run on sterling, then invest
As the pound plummets—smart!

Old firms collapse at their behest,
Job-markets fall apart,
And whole economies go west
As brokers fix the chart.

The one percent conceive they're blest
To practise that black art
While the poor folk they've second-guessed
Lose fortunes, then lose heart.

The big shots say 'we've passed the test,
Got game-plans *à la carte*,
So don't blame us if you, the rest,
Still scan 'Exchange and Mart'!

4

Our new-style PM is a man
As worthy as can be:
He's worth more hundred million than
The crookedest lawyer's fee.

And yet he's worthless, one who can
Be counted on to see
Those lawless lawyers serve his plan—
They'll fettle lock to key!

Think how he has the tabloids pan
Our every move to free
Their captive readers from the ban
On any conscience-plea.

He'll have his minions tip the pan
Of justice so that we
Should not go on as we began,
True friends of liberty.

He'll stitch us up, he and his clan
Who bend a servile knee
To no god but the god who ran
Their fixers' lottery.

5

These new-style Tories ply their trade
In pink shirts, ties and suits;
They spurn the old-style boast 'self-made'
And stash their cash with Coutts.

Peas in a pod, that suit-parade,
Poor crop with cankered roots,
PM and cronies on parade—
All fraudsters in cahoots.

And should you ask 'How shall we grade
His kind?, then 'by their fruits!'
Is how, or by the guile displayed
In faked-up 'woke' disputes.

6

'Investment banker'—how that tag
Runs through him like a stick
Of Brighton rock—he's out to bag
The grifter's prize, first pick!

In moral terms there's no old lag
Has such a list to tick
As sins recalled conspire to drag
His time out in the nick.

Pure dog-eat-dog stuff, that's his bag,
His money-spinning shtick;
When other bankers' fortunes sag
He moves in—that's the trick!

Should someone spot a moral snag
He shuts them up dead quick
Or slaps some hefty legal gag
On them in half a tick.

7

'Investment banker': how the phrase
Consigns him to perdition,
Though there's an apter role it plays
If placed in rhyme-position!

Let's blame a blocked-up anal phase
For making it his mission
To see the hated Other pays
For that long-stalled transition.

You seek the root of this malaise?
Best ask a soul-physician
Since she's the one who'll best appraise
His zombie-like condition.

Behold him: adman's vacant gaze
And Colgate-bright dentition,
A tv popinjay who sprays
It on for each transmission.

8

That's what you'll get each time you vote
Them in, those city guys;
A Gucci heel-mark on your throat
And warnings to the wise.

Hard times? 'We're all in the same boat'—
That slogan they devise
To calm unrest then thieve the float
To show how it applies,

Like many a phrase they like to quote
And all the proven lies
Their tabloid celebrants promote
So backers advertise.

Just look and listen, simply note
The groomed look, shifty eyes,
Bespoke suit (natch), and got-by-rote
Response: try this for size!

9

There's wicked, and there's evil, but
Those terms don't fit the bill,
Though, god knows, he'd not bust a gut
To stop them doing ill,

Those sicko mates of his who shut
Their eyes when migrants spill
From fragile boats, or colleagues strut
Their stuff and thieve their fill.

No, he's a blank, a monsters' mutt,
A man who lacks the will,
The wit, the nerve to raise a 'tut'
When they rouse to the kill.

Maybe he'll pause while flunkies cut
His hair—that daily thrill—
Glance in the glass, and sense the glut
Of lives gone out like swill.

10

But what's the chance he'd then condole
With them, begin to fret
At what he's done?—poor, on the whole,
And surely no sign yet!

Those old-school Tories played the role
Of grisly gargoyles set
In some dark niche to fright the soul
With their blood-chilling threat.

These new ones show more self-control
And wouldn't deign to let
Things go by some perverse own-goal
Or breach of etiquette.

No, for it seems the latest poll
Says there's more votes to get
By ways that tell the cash-strapped prole
'We'll get you out of debt',

While he, with heated water-hole
And much-used private jet,
Adds daily to the pile he stole
With all expenses met.

11

Orwell was right in this at least:
The country is a mess,
Like some old family prone to feast
On dreams of past *noblesse*.

All the wrong sorts in charge, palms greased
To save unpleasantness,
And junior members well policed
To keep it from the press

While paterfamilias, a beast
Still garbed in evening dress,
Complained all day how he'd been fleeced
By peasants *sans finesse*.

So it goes now, except they've ceased
To suffer such distress,
Those idlers, since their wealth increased
Beyond their wildest guess.

Yet it's still *Downton Abbey*, pieced
Together by success
At nothing more than greed released
To cheat and dispossess.

From London and all points South-East
The rich folk stand to bless
Their saviours, though it's 'Judas Priest!'
The working folk profess.

'Enough's Enough' Song

(to be sung to the tune of 'The Gay Gordons' or any song with the same measures)

O we've had enough of the ruling class,
We've had enough of their tricks,
So we'll put the Tories out to grass
And knock the bosses for six.
Enough's enough, enough's enough,
We'll not put up with it now.
Enough's enough, enough's enough,
We're gonna show them how!

O we've had enough of the profiteers,
The bankers, bilkers and cheats;
It's our wage-arrears coming out of their ears
And they want us off the streets!
Enough's enough, the system's duff,
We've had it with Kwarteng and Truss.
If they think a kick in the teeth's enough,
Then they haven't reckoned with us!

O we've had enough of the management lies,
The tale they always concoct
When it's them lined up for a salary-rise
And us whose wages are docked.
Enough's enough, enough's enough,
We've had it right up to here.
We want some smooth to go with the rough
And we're not gonna disappear!

O we've had enough of our union reps
Being shown the boardroom door,
And we think it's time we took some steps
To see that it happens no more!
Enough's enough, enough's enough,

The bosses are at it again;
They hoist the ladder when times are tough
And tell us our pleas are in vain.
Now we've had it with sleazy CEOs,
And we've had it with Tory MPs,
And we've had it with all the cash that flows
From our pockets so they live at ease.
Enough's enough, enough's enough,
We'll give the bankers a shock
When the union tells them where to stuff
That 1-percent voting stock!

Yes, 'enough's enough' is the cry that resounds
Through the factories, fields, and farms
Where the Levellers' message is doing the rounds
And the words are a call-to-arms.
'Enough's enough' of the same old bluff,
The same old fiddler's tune,
For the bosses will find they've had enough
Of 'enough's enough' very soon!

In Whose Bad Books?

1

Our pastor, he said 'Praise the Lord,
Give praise unto His name,
And spread the gospel news abroad:
To save your souls He came!'.

He said 'The grapes of wrath are stored
For those who bear the blame
That drags us mortals hellfire-ward
To feed the Devil's flame'.

I harkened, took it all on board,
And told my kids 'For shame,
Listen up else you'll be zero-scored
When God decides the game'.

But then I thought: 'There's things ignored
In all that he'd proclaim,
Things apt to strike a jarring chord
With folk outside the frame.

2

That Jesus, he had stuff to say
That goes for black and white,
Good news our pastor could convey
And help set old wrongs right.

You know, the bits not only they
But us black folks can cite
Because there ain't no earthly way
They'll spread the racist blight.

Truth, justice, peace on earth—let's pray
Those words shed kindly light
And quench the flame whose kindling may
Burn fierce in darkest night.

A good man, Jesus, when he'd play
It down, that touch of spite
That blasted the fig-tree to pay
Those chatterers back alright!

3

But Christ-as-God's the one who'll see
You burn in Hell should you
Risk any word or deed that He
Deems wicked or taboo.

Old monks devised the Trinity
In hopes that it might do
To silence such rank heresy
Amongst the errant crew.

Still look around and you'll agree:
It's God, not Christ, that slew
Those legions of the damned whose plea
The wrong God listened to.

The one to whom they bend the knee,
The God of Soldier Blue,
Is He whose old book's held to be
The sole book good and true.

It holds the one and only key,
The single passe-partout
Vouchsafed by Him to guarantee
They pay the homage due.

And when the tribal lords decree
Some holy war or new
Crusade to wage they'll soon make free
With Joshua's hullabaloo.

I hear it in their hymnody,
With our old pastor, too,
When he takes such unChristian glee
In tales of butchery.

It's in the blood-filled oratory,
The martial tropes on cue,
The monotheists' battle-spree
To get a God's-eye view.

4

But nearer home I saw it fill
The airwaves, tv screens,
And op eds: 'they went out to kill,
Those two black female teens.

A woman elderly and ill
They killed by brutal means,
A Bible teacher who'd instil
God's grace in wolverines.

Don't blame their parents' lack of skill,
Don't blame it on their genes,
Don't say it's what their home-lives drill
Them into—death-machines!

No, we'll not walk safe streets until
We've junked those childhood scenes
Of violence, want, and horrorsville
So justice intervenes.

5

For the Lord tells us: eye-for-eye
And tooth-for-tooth's the law,
And those two girls have got to die
To quit the moral score'.

That's what he said, the lawyer guy,
And the DA then swore
That it would anger God on high
If sins weren't answered for.

It's how they think, the folk who buy
That vengeful line—what more
Effective way to block the cry
Of conscience they ignore?

It's him, the Moloch-god, who'll pry
Into the hate-filled core
Of minds long driven far awry
By that god-awful lore.

Those old books have the sinners fry,
And their god wipe the floor
With infidels who dare to try
The penalties in store.

O there's good bits, you can't deny,
Like passages that soar
On prophet-wings to touch the sky
Or heaven's gleaming shore.

Yet always there's some sinner nigh,
Some tribe to shock and awe,
Or angel to touch Jacob's thigh:
'Not yours but God's, this war!'.

Our pastor has his own supply
Of bible-quotes he'll draw
So swiftly on you never spy
Some massacre in the raw.

But that's the itch they satisfy,
The itch of tooth and claw
To hear him conjure deeds we'd shy
From once through the church-door.

6

And now each latest bulletin
From Gaza lets us know
Once more how massacres begin
When preachers run the show.

The same old talk—'wages of sin',
'God's children' or 'God's foe',
'We chosen ones', 'you devil's kin',
And suchlike to-and-fro.

It's still the same old tales they spin,
The tales that strike a blow
For each hate-manual and its twin—
Two creeds, same war-tableaux.

Sometimes I think the guys who'd pin
The death-rap on those low-
Life scapegoat girls are mirrored in
The siege of Jericho,

Since that's the mythic origin
Of what the victims owe
To bible-lore when victors win
On points scored long ago.

The truth 'all one beneath the skin,
All kindred, bro and bro',
Gets lost each time the trumpets' din
Brings yet more grief and woe.

For it's the vengeful god within
That answers when they blow
And spike some war-primed endorphin
With carnage to bestow

7

I catch the bible-bashing tone
In that DA's appeal
For the death-sentence to be thrown
At girls too hurt to heal.

I catch it in the battle-zone
Reports of those whose zeal
For far-off kills by bomb or drone
They're hard-put to conceal.

But you've a language all your own,
You holy men who deal
In sanctifying missions flown
Or fusillades of steel.

It's your God churns the flesh and bone,
Whips up the hate they feel,
His chosen ones, or sees them blown
To bits unless they kneel.

He taunts the victims as they groan
On the inquisitor's wheel,
And tells his flock 'Let them atone
Beneath the Seventh Seal'.

For it's a savage seed they've sown,
Those scriptures that reveal
Depths of malignity unknown
Till blind faith makes them real.

Conservative Thinkers: thirty clerihews

Thomas Hobbes
So feared violent mobs
That he wrote *De Cive*
To leave them no leeway.

***

Edmund Burke
Said revolt couldn't work –
Told a sanguinary story
So we wouldn't vote Tory.

***

Pitt the Elder
Is thought to have held a
Deep grudge toward George III,
Who heartily concurred.

Pitt the Younger
Was a great power-monger,
A description that fits
Son and Dad—it's the Pitts!

***

Benjamin Disraeli
Took time off daily
So that he could scribble
A few lines of *Sybil*.

***

Alexis de Tocqueville
Thought the US was Shockville
While lifting his hat
To the word 'democrat'.

Let's not say hypocrisy
But a sense of 'democracy'
Not overly inclined
To keep poor folk in mind.

***

Otto von Bismarck
Knew how to leave *his* mark
On German history:
Kick-start it—no mystery!

Still his reputation
As saviour of the nation
Came under strain
When he annexed Alsace-Lorraine.

***

Thomas Carlyle
Had the hectoring style
To beat Robert de Niro's
Swashbuckling heroes.

***

Lord Acton
Never once slacked on
His big theme: state power
Made free men cower.

***

Roger Scruton
Wouldn't sit on a futon—
Said 'Chesterfield settee
Or nothing for me!'.

***

Leo Strauss
Kept a bawdy-house.
One rule: that all punters
Be subtext-hunters.

***

Robert Nozick
Was quite virtuosic
At dating girls late
In his night-watchman state.

***

Ayn Rand
Was a bit underhand
In ensuring they plugged
Atlas Shrugged.

***

Irving Kristol
Jumped the starter's pistol:
In no time he'd gone
From far-left to neo-con.

**

Friedman, Milton
Said justice was built on
Robin Hood in reverse:
Stuff the rich guy's purse!

**

Friedrich von Hayek
Told his followers 'By heck,
We'll get them to junk
All that socialist bunk'.

**

William F. Buckley
Was unarmed, luckily –
Else Vidal-gore
Might have spattered the floor.

**

T.S. Eliot, poet,
Said 'Feeling? Don't show it—
What you happen to feel
Is no big deal'.

Besides, Thomas Stearns
Thought private concerns
Needn't get their old hook in
Once God got a look-in.

'If the peanut gallery
Roots for Viv, then Valerie
Can use the *Cats* cash
To settle their hash.'

Thus the blessed T.S.,
Now freed from all stress,
Bade his muse: 'Now let's
Write my *Four Quartets*!'.

       ***

Anthony Quinton
Looked somewhat asquint on
The least sign or token
Of college-rules broken.

       ***

Alasdair MacIntyre
Was a great supplier
Of antique faith-recliners,
Main source: Aquinas.

       ***

Hark awhile to John Gray:
He's some dark things to say,
But don't listen too hard
Or you'll be psychically scarred.

       ***

Maurice Cowling
Set the liberals howling,
Though Enoch and Co.
Gave his ideas a go.

All the high-table scowling
And dog-whistle Powelling
Went down a treat
With the Peterhouse elite.

***

Raymond Aron
Steered clear of a bar on
The heights of Montmartre
Frequented by Sartre.

***

Dinesh D'Souza's
The scourge of all losers,
Hispanic or black:
Well, he's all right, Jack!

***

Jacob Rees-Mogg
Got it on with a dog,
Who complied, duly heeding
His superior breeding.

***

Ferdinand Mount
Said 'On no account
Give my books a bad press
(Signed: Editor, *TLS*)'.

Pablo Neruda: late thoughts

Political poetry is more profoundly emotional than any other—at least as much
as love poetry—and cannot be forced because it then becomes vulgar and
unacceptable. It is necessary first to pass through all other poetry in order to
become a political poet. The political poet must also be prepared to accept the
censure which is thrown at him—betraying poetry, or betraying literature.
Then, too, political poetry has to arm itself with such content and substance
and intellectual and emotional richness that it is able to scorn everything else.
This is rarely achieved.

—Pablo Neruda, interview with Rita Guibert, *The Paris Review*

Impure, I said, keep poetry impure,
Find room for everything, warm woollen socks,
Old suits, tomatoes, onions, stuff to cure

The lyric-warbling Romeo who mocks
The humdrum clutter of our daily lives
Just as he likes to keep a tight-sealed box

Marked 'Politics—Beware!' so love survives
Untouched by all the squalor, broken vows,
And treachery on which it feeds and thrives,

The savage twist of fortune that allows
Allende's overthrow when Pinochet,
Our vile dictator, gets to figure now's

The time to seize his chance the nearest way,
Bring forward the promised coup, and see me dead
Along with thousands more. The doctors say

It's prostate cancer, that the things's now spread
To other parts, and that I've barely time
For a few calls from this hospital bed

Before it does me in. But just think: I'm
Back, pretty much, to my old body-weight
With most bits functioning as in my prime,

Those vital bits included, so if fate
Has this day singled out for my demise
Then chances are it's not by the dictate

Of a slow-creeping, long ignored disease
That it's come round but by the swift decree
Of that swine Pinochet who knows that he's

Got everything to lose if he lets me,
The people's poet, make it to the plane
That's waiting for me and—as he'll say—'flee

The country just to save his skin again
And get those commie Mexicans onside'.
It's not the cancer, not this latest pain,

So fierce, so localised, here where they tried
Three times today to stick that needle in,
Then managed. Rumour says another died

In this same room, and—maybe just the spin
Folk put on it—a few hours after he'd,
Like me, had that strange medic crew come in

Quite unannounced and rapidly proceed
To do the same to him with, as I fear,
Much the same likelihood that it would lead

To much the same result. And now I hear
The radio's put it out that I'd die soon
While Pinochet's been overheard to sneer

At 'how the pinko bard will change his tune
When his plane plummets flaming from the sky
En route for Mexico this afternoon

And he's at last obliged to kiss goodbye
To his wild dream of getting them on board,
Diego Rivera, that Picasso guy,

And all the arty-farty-lefty horde,
Along with all the dumb Latinos sold
On socialist ideas they can't afford

This side of Shangri-La'.
        That's what he told
Me, my chauffeur who sometimes drives the gang
Of psychopaths that Pinochet's enrolled

As bodyguards so I soon got the hang
Of it, how they'd arrange to have me killed
In one way or another, final bang

Or massive shot of thallium. Else I'd build
The kind of opposition that could screw
Things up for him if poetry fulfilled

Its highest task and promise: to renew
The long-dishonoured covenant between
Those who have means enough, the lucky few,

And those, the dispossessed, whose lives I've seen
Close-up, and shared, and who themselves once shared
Their home and hearth with me as if I'd been

Some poem-spouting prodigal who'd erred,
Left home behind, then come back having learned
What further harms and dangers he'd been spared

By that good choice. It's why my poems turned
From *eros* to—how should I say?—perhaps
A form of *agape* that can't be earned

By prayer, or faith, or checking every lapse
From grace, but only comes by leaving such
Soul-pilgrimages off our mental maps

And finding how to kick away the crutch
Of any spooky creed that stakes its claim
To wisdom far beyond the common touch

Of human kindness. This they showed who came
To save me soul and body way back when
I knocked and woke them, those to whom my name

Meant nothing yet for whom this least of men,
This wild-eyed fugitive, required they set
Safety or self-concern aside and then,

Just like that, take me in. So please don't get
Me wrong on this: it's eros still that stirs
My soul to song and grabs my sluggish pen

When *agape* too readily concurs
With that bleak estimate of humankind
So tellingly conveyed by my chauffeur's

Too-late attempt to put me well in mind
Of what those killers planned. Presume to raise
Your sights too high and you'll most likely find

You overshoot the human mark in ways
That range from plain inept to downright bad,
Or let's say: from the archangelic gaze

That skips small mishaps to the armour-clad
Battalions Pinochet's already got
Lined up in his mind's eye. Like Galahad,

But minus the round-table knightly lot
Who now—perhaps already then, who knows?—
Are just the types you'd more expect to spot

At some ID parade or amongst those
CIA-sponsored, IBM-financed
Conspirators who ganged up to depose

And kill Allende just because he danced
To measures more uplifting, more attuned
To human needs and hopes than those advanced

By 'national salvation budgets' pruned
Of all but corporate pelf.
                    'Let me explain',
I once wrote, 'why my poems aren't festooned

With lilies, roses, and that heartfelt strain
Of lyric, love-fixated metaphors
I once enjoyed, but press against the grain

Of any verse that in these times still draws
On figures, themes and sentiments more apt
To conjure passive dreaming than to cause,

In grounded readers, passions yet untapped
For love and justice. Love that re-unites
The sundered soul and body in a rapt

Though passionate communion that indicts
A loveless world, and justice that would rest
Content with no world where the body's rights

To earthly pleasures have to meet the test
Of forced compliance with the soul's regime
Of quashed desires, or at the state's behest

Each time some Pinochet thinks up a scheme
To track and kill the *promesse de bonheur*
Made good by every *eros*-granted dream

That liberated bodies may confer
On love-starved souls. It's the same psychic twist
That drives that constant need of his to slur

My poems like my politics, insist
That such 'obscene' eroticism taints
The poet's sacred calling, and enlist

His gangs to reinforce the chaste constraints
(With thumbscrews if required) that go to make
The world safe for enervate poet-saints

Or citizens persuaded to forsake
The way of revolution for a taste
Of sugared honey. It's their pauper's stake

In every bit of dirty business based
On CIA connections, crooked deals,
And contract killings such as I'd have faced

For sure if I'd not taken to my heels
And found salvation from the cynic's snare
In all the hideouts, sleeping-places, meals,

And, more than anything, the risks they'd dare
Take on for me, a stranger. That's what kept
Me going, fought it off, the old despair

At human guile and treachery that crept
Up on me when I thought of how he stole
Their land and lives, how crook-financiers swept

Their hard-earned savings into some black hole
Of US corporate thievery, and how
Nothing was safe, in bank or begging-bowl,

Once IBM had fixed things. They'd allow
The Wall Street moguls, hedge-fund hikers, plus
Those mates of his with one eye on the Dow

To get most money flowing with least fuss
From cash-strapped peasantry to men for whom
We'd matter not a jot, the likes of us,

Since capital has precious little room
For those, the victims and the sons of toil,
Who suffer just as much from bust or boom,

Whose untold pains and labours go to oil
The wheels of capital, and who alone,
If they but knew, have strength and means to spoil

The lurching juggernaut. I'll make it known,
That truth suppressed by every servile hack
Or sold-out jobbing journalist who'll atone

For one lie with another, every pack
Of profit-hungry speculators, each
New banker with portfolio to stack

Against the folk whose livelihoods he'll leech
Away through market-fixing. Plus—to cap
This grim recital—every judge who'll preach

A courtroom sermon full of pious crap
About the law's neutrality and zeal
That good men thrive while villains take the rap

Yet inwardly rejoice at what a steal
It's been, this latest Pinochet-backed ruse
To have the peasantry devoutly kneel

Before Judge Mammon and prepare to lose
Whatever dignity they'd once enjoyed
As bringers-home of wages they could use

For life's necessities. They're rendered void
Of their old buying-power through the malign
Effect of galloping inflation buoyed

By market-savvy judges who'd consign
The Chilean people to a lingering death
Before they'd think of calling out the swine

Whose currency transactions choked the breath
Of those who took me in.
                I hear them ask
Again: 'Why make this your new shibboleth,

This thought of justice as the poet's task,
Not love as in those poems that so struck
A generation eager to unmask

Old falsities and call a fuck a fuck,
Yet do so through a language that enshrined
The act of love in images you'd pluck

Not from some high Platonic realm refined
Beyond all sensuous apprehension but
From loving bodies sensuously entwined,

Legs, arms, thighs, breasts, and all the wondrous glut
Of human sexuality?'. This brings
It home, by vivid contrast, how tight-shut

They soon become to every joy that springs
From uncoerced desires, that fascist crew
Of his along with victims, underlings,

Wives, children—all the hate-filled retinue
Of such a man. They suffer its reprise
In each once natural instinct forced askew

By the neurotic mind-and-body squeeze
Of thwarted need, blocked passion, sex gone wrong,
And the dark aftermath (think Sophocles!)

Of some perverse compulsion to prolong
And deepen every lethal drive instilled
When passion's turbid current runs so strong

That no verse-offering innocently billed
'Love-Poem' should protest at being classed
'Escapist trash' except amongst the guild

Of hungover romantics. They contrast
The 'old' Neruda, celebrant of all
Things delicate yet destined to outlast

The greatest empires, with what now they call
My sadly frequent tendency to give
That lyric strain short shrift and promptly fall

To treating themes as crass or fugitive
As fill the daily news. Why squander your
True gift and have us doubt those lines that live

And breathe love's vibrant truth by opting for
The transient, grubby world of politics
Where there's no once love-hallowed metaphor

But's then besmirched, defiled, or forced to mix
With trivial faits *divers'*.
           I tell them: think
Of Victor Jara, how he could transfix

The listener with his love-songs, how they'd link
Minds, hearts and souls by that combined effect
Of poetry with music's power to shrink

A lifeworld into lyrics that reflect
Not just one lover's joys or fond regret
But, always there, the way these moods connect

With social passions and contrive to get
His message out. No state of strife or peace
In love's domain without some larger threat

Or chance of happiness that might release
Just such a charge of fear and hope as finds
Expression in his songs. When lovers cease

To write them or when listeners close their minds
To what those love-songs also have to tell,
If read aright, concerning humankind's

Political condition, this could spell
One of two things: utopia, an end
To enmity and strife, or—quite as well—

The end of categories like foe or friend
Since no one any longer has the will,
Strength, courage or commitment to contend

With enemies they'd back then seek to kill
But now can't raise their spirits to engage
Once more. That's even when they've had their fill

Of hearkening to some jumped-up bar-room sage
Who tells them Pinochet's the man with wads
Of cash to buy the judges, turn a page

In Chile's glorious history, let the squads
Of AK-47-touting goons
Sniff treason out, and save the land for God's

Main man Augusto and his tame buffoons
To share between them. Think of how he sang,
My comrade Victor, when the words and tunes

Still spoke of love although the kidnap gang
Had dragged him off for torture, the abyss
Had opened up before us, and the pang

Of unrequited passion or the bliss
Of dreams fulfilled took on, as in my verse,
A covert, sinister dimension: kiss

Of life or kiss of death? blessing or curse?
In evil times like these even love may show
Itself in unfamiliar forms or, worse,

Be so distorted, twisted, made to go
Such tortured, self-destructive ways around
That, should some further check obstruct the flow,

Then every last frail flood-defence is drowned
By the pent violence hiding, tightly coiled,
In men and movements now destruction-bound

And fed by all the thwarted drives embroiled
In all the histories of eros skewed
Off-course or high hopes by low motives foiled

And turned into a monstrous multitude
At one sick tyrant's call.
                    Yet that's no cause
For poets or idealists to brood

Too much on what's revealed of human flaws,
Infirmities, and outright wickedness
By Chile's case and think some hideous law's

At work there as in every age, or stress,
Like Shakespeare's sonnet, how the pure in heart
Are often those whom evil may possess

Most deeply since their moral reckonings start
From zero worldly knowledge and too soon
Conclude that learning-curves should all depart

From that point, then foresee a future strewn,
Like Walter Benjamin's, with wreckage piled
Sky-high each time the latest kill-platoon

Swarms out to hit the streets. Yes, they defiled
So much of what we built together, thanks
To that great man Allende, till he riled

The Wall Street brokers, money-markets, banks,
And all the death-squads kept on high alert
By those old friends of liberty, the Yanks,

Whenever something happened that might hurt
Their own financial interests. Yet if that
Still sparks your zeal for justice, why desert

Your comrades now, why let the autocrat
Succeed in his design so every two-
Bit gangster-type will stage a *coup d'etat*

Then call their mates and fixers in to screw
The people over, sell the country out,
And see that Chile gets the credit due

For showing how a bit of mobster-clout
Like his can bring a country to its knees
If those who won its freedom come to doubt

The good of all they fought for, or appease
Their consciences by thinking *did our bit*
Back then—now it's for you, the young, to seize

Your chance and fight again. They'll pass it off,
That taunt, by saying *OK Pablo, spare*
Us yet more sermonising: best not scoff

Too much at our expense now you've your share
Of money, fame, and all the adulation
A man could ask for, plus—let's add, since their

Experiences sometimes shocked the nation—
The many women, wife or girlfriends, whose
Love-fortunes touched your own at some life-station

Though boarding-points and stops were yours to choose
While they were lucky if they got enough
Press coverage through the break-ups not to lose

The public's sympathy. The times were tough,
For them at least, though you had your Nobel
(Deserved, no doubt) to offset all the stuff

Like that poor Tamil maid who learned too well
The brutal truth: that starring roles were short-
Term only and that, once the curtain fell,

The only question was how best support
Neruda, he whose poetry inspired
A people to take arms and rouse the court

Of natural justice to a conscience fired
By his example. So the charge-sheet runs,
I know, and can't just say 'they're scoundrels hired

By Pinochet or soul-corrupted sons-
Of-bitches who'll be quick to cut a deal
With any hack who'll give the hired guns

Their pretext to abandon the genteel,
Time-honoured civil code and just get down
To sorting this lot out'. I'll set no seal

Of 'right to privacy', nor go to town
On how those goons of his elect to bandy
Such stuff around as if thereby to crown

A case that picks up any factoid handy
For their campaign to turn the folk against
A man they'd treat as one more poet-dandy,

No longer somehow sacrosanct or fenced
Off by decree behind the mythic props
That held up just so long as folk dispensed

With asking: what's left once the penny drops
And Pablo's cover's blown?
       I'll not dispute
The facts, nor ask what role the Special Ops

Detachment played in digging dirt to suit
The General's purpose. Yes, that 'sexist' hook's
Not easily wriggled off as some astute

PR man might suppose, or one who looks
To image over substance, like that bunch
Of Nobel judges who'd have closed their books

On me for good as downright out to lunch
Politically for having penned an Ode
To Josef Stalin and borne out their hunch

That I was just some commie on the road
To serfdom. So their guru Hayek told
The demagogues and juntas who kowtowed

To capital and saw their people sold
Into wage-slavery rather than defend
Those human rights and freedoms placed on hold

In profit's sovereign name. You'll say I bend
The case my way, do what I've always done,
Draw once more on the long-banked dividend

Of my old glory-days and tales I've spun
So often to avert the other sorts
Of question, those self-interest bids me shun

Except (believe me!) when my small-hour thoughts
Creep back. Then I, like my accusers, know
They can't be laid to rest by more reports

Of brave deeds, poems fit to overthrow
A nest of tyrants, and—but you've rehearsed
The whole back-story for me, blow by blow—

How it was my *Cancion General* that first
Showed how the Latin peoples might conceive
Their destinies beyond the ages cursed

To suffer the imperial by-your-leave
And look to those brave futures manifest
In what its people dreamed they might achieve

Yet, as my Cancion let them know, expressed
In ways invisible to those who knew
Only which one to choose should they invest

In local produce strictly with a view
To high returns.
              Yes, *yes*—again I've blinked,
Allowed the poet-hero stuff to slew

What I must now confess, clear and distinct:
Not only those liaisons, broken vows,
A wife betrayed, the Tamil maid . . . all linked,

Perversely, with whatever had me rouse
My people to those liberating heights
Of national awareness and espouse

The common cause of human needs and rights,
For Chile most directly, to be sure,
But beyond that for everyone who fights

The tyranny of capital, the lure
Of US-sponsored thieves and killers trained
To seek out those weak vessels who'd abjure

Their hard-won freedoms for whatever's gained
By selling Chilean silver on the cheap
For thirty pieces of the same stuff strained

Through treachery's Yankee sieve. One thing I keep
Repeating to myself when conscience calls
In the small hours and old misgivings creep

Up on me yet again: those know-it-alls
And gossip-columnists who so rejoice
In judging me might ask themselves what balls

It took to write those early lovers'-choice
Poems of mine where love, desire, and lust
(Ideally three-in-one) found their true voice

And, equally, those where the lover's trust
In goodness, truth, and beauty had succumbed
To the grim knowledge that these matters must

Yield place when poets speak to souls benumbed
By such harsh torments as the people bore
And suffer still. It's those damned legions drummed

Up by the tinpot General and his core
Of thugs and mercenaries with snouts
All stuck in what's, for them, the tax-free store

Of Chile's silver mines. Such turnabouts
Were once the lot of poets way back when
Their courtly-love songs likewise suffered bouts

Of war, plague, famine, vassalage, and pen
Exchanged for sword, as well as all the much-
Lamented woes endured by love-sick men

At fictive women's hands.
            Time was I'd clutch
At some such saving phantasy in modes
Petrarchan or Platonic, but it's Dutch

(Forgive me!) courage that can bear no loads
Beyond the slightest obstacle on love's
Uneven, always treacherous open roads

Through territory where any god above's
Either a stupid cupid or a being
Supreme in nothing but push-come-to shove's

Old rule: that no all-knowing or all-seeing
Love-deity can play a more than stand-
In, rubber-stamping role by just agreeing

To fate's obscure decrees, nor countermand
One jot of its prevision. That's the tale
They all fall back on, that deluded band

Of old-school lovers, once the visions fail,
The myths are demythologised, and there's
This truth to face: that both can lead to gaol

Or death, the love of woman that prepares
A man to risk his soul for what transcends
Self-interest, and the stake he thereby shares

With the entire community that lends
All those who fight in freedom's cause a worth
Beyond romantic love yet comprehends

That, too, amongst the goods of mother earth
We strive for. See life whole and then we could,
In time, find ways to remedy the dearth

Of love, truth, beauty, and true nationhood
That they, the likes of Pinochet, contrive
So as to keep us blind to all that would,

Once glimpsed, do untold wonders to revive
Those cherished hopes and raise our downcast eyes
To a new Chile where the just would thrive

While tyrants, bankers, company agents, spies,
And all the devil's spawn who joined to cause
Our nation's grief and helped the brute devise

His killing spree would find their bloody claws
Pulled by its victims from the tight-clenched fist
That wrought those horrors.
              No exemption-clause

For me, the poet or the fantasist
In me who thought—simplistically—that my
Deep passion-fired love-lyrics might enlist

A mass of freedom-fired recruits, untie
The mess of tangled motives, and afford
Their lives, like mine, what men were guided by

When words cut clean and swiftly as a sword
Through the best-armoured lies of those who'd bribe,
Twist, threaten, kill, and thereby get to lord

It over those who'll readily imbibe
Whatever's fed them by the plutocrats,
The gunmen, and the new sharp-suited tribe

Of big-time mobsters keen to raise their hats
To our blood-soaked dictator. I'll confess:
There's much about my life that those expats

Can point to and suggest you re-assess
'The legend of Neruda', take due stock
Of all my faults and weaknesses, or press

The charge that's often stood me in the dock
Of 'public morals', summoned there by tools
Of US trade and Chilean banks in hock

To the same expat syndicate that drools
On each new 'revelation' of how base
My treatment of 'his women', and that schools

The cub reporters in where best to place
Their shock reports. If, finally, this reads
Like one more try to ward off that disgrace,

As if half-consciously, by one who needs
A reflex alibi then let me state
The case outright lest indirection leads

To 'guilty by default'. You underrate,
You self-appointed judges, what it took
To write those poems (time was, they'd castrate

Such plain-truth tellers out of nature's book!),
Or what joint craft and inspiration went
To stir the deep-laid passions that so shook

Not only lovers with their heightened bent
For heart's desires thus shaken but, beyond
That charmed domain, the latent discontent

Or long-repressed frustrations that respond
To communal injustices and wrongs
State-sponsored and designed to fray the bond

Of mutual trust and amity that songs
And poetry may hope to disinfest
Of vermin through the passion that belongs

As much to love as politics.
   'I rest
My case', I'd say, except that it's the kind
Of case that can't be summed up till we're blessed

With a new sense of how desire can blind
Us, sometimes, yet at other times may prove
The only force that bids we leave behind

A loveless life, a vile regime, a groove
Where wish-fulfilment placidly pursues
Its normal course till earth and stars should move

Their orbits or some power, prophet or muse,
Command a change as radical as goes
To bring love's *vita nuova*, or enthuse

A captive people to renounce the prose
Of their quotidian lives. Then they might cast
Off every metric fashioned to foreclose

The poetry that else might lead them past
The tyranny of the everyday or life
As lived within the citadel held fast

By the cash-nexus. Talk of man and wife,
Like every human bond, as chief among
The victims here may seem to twist the knife

In my own heart, what with the charges hung
Part-justly on me since the erstwhile myth
Of Pablo, poet-saviour, that once clung

To me's no longer one to conjure with,
Whether as hope revived for those who've borne
Their sufferings long enough or as the pith

Of all they fear in me, those traitors sworn
To root out and destroy the very source
Of hope in words they'd have the people scorn

Since uttered by a no-good whose divorce
And 'love-intrigues' they scorned. Behold those fine
Upholders of a rule that would endorse

Iniquities galore yet call divine
Requital down to vindicate the code
Of 'family values', taken as a sign

Of full compliance with the duty owed
To church, state, army, Pinochet, and what-
Soever new indignities he'd load

On acquiescent souls. That some things blot
The copy-books of those who had the luck,
Be it good or bad, to live in just the spot

At just the hour when history's timepiece struck
The fateful hour should surely rate more . . . . let's
Say tolerance, or insight, than the ruck

Of media hacks provide since nothing whets
The jaded appetite of readers keen
On such salacious gossip like what gets

Some culture-hero driven to demean
Himself by answering charges all the more
Insidious since concerning what's off-screen

From public view, involves no rule of law,
And hence allows me no defence or way
To prove my case or level that old score

With my detractors. Still this much I'll say:
My poems are the best of me, and they'll
Speak up for me, bear witness, not betray

What you, my readers, shared with me—that tale,
Part-told, as yet unfinished, of how we,
The people, found love-songs to countervail

The goose-step songs of hate, how spirits free
Might conquer spirits cowed, and how words scrawled
In haste by one pursued could later be

A source of hope for many when recalled
By countless victims as they come to see,
There imaged, loves and lifetimes disenthralled
From all that's scarred our country's history.

Trussturcluck—fifteen clerihews

Prime Minister

The Rt Hon Liz Truss
Has caused quite a fuss.
That's why, as PM,
She's strictly pro tem.

       ***

Chancellor of the Exchequer

Mr Kwasi Kwarteng
Loves a bit of ginseng.
Tax-free in his budget—
A fiddle, we judge it!

       ***

Business Secretary

Mr Jacob Rees-Mogg
Seems a gay young dog,
Though still doting on Nanny
At fifty—uncanny!

       ***

Deputy Prime Minister

Thérèse Coffey
Just loves toffee.
This no doubt explains
Her varicose veins.

       ***

Foreign Secretary

Mr Cleverly, James,
Has a thing about names.
Hence the stiff gin-and-tonic
When folk say 'how ironic!'.

***

'Defence' Secretary

That fine chap Ben Wallace
Finds war a great solace.
Must know what the toll is—
Now God help the polis!

***

Chancellor of the Duchy of Lancaster

Mr Nadhim Zahawi—
'Equalities', are we?
Levelling up, the sequel:
You plebs stay unequal!

***

Leader of the House of Commons

Ms Penny Mordaunt
Strikes a note most discordant.
Virtues: not many.
Boasts: two-a-penny.

***

Home Secretary

Braverman, Suella—
Please, someone tell her
Rear-end gravitas
Shows the law's an ass.

**

International Trade Secretary

Kemi Badenoch
Says she's had enough
Of asking 'Who is
This Brandon Lewis?'.

(answer: Justice Secretary!)

**

Levelling Up and Housing Secretary

Simon Clarke
Thought 'What a lark:
The plebs need rousing—
Let's screw up Housing!'.

**

Conservative Party Chairman

Said Chairman Jake
(Gilchrist) Berry:
Sure, we're on the make—
Eat, drink, be merry!

**

Scotland Secretary

Poor Alister Jack—
Soon be seeing his back
As he crosses the border
In short order.

***

Chief Whip

Name: Wendy Morton.
Career: a short'un,
Though sure to have grossed
A pile when in post.

***

Hanger-On and Pop-Up TV Clown

John Redwood, MP,
Told grandson: 'you'll see
Them mock me again, lad,
Lip-syncing 'Mae Hen Gwlad'.

Isms: a taxonomy

Those isms run the gamut A to ZED
But come in one or other sort:
The types that claim your credence, fill your head,
And yield doctrinal memes to spread,
Or sundry ills and ailments of the kind
You've somehow—bloody nuisance!—caught
But which, with luck, won't touch your heart or mind.

There's all those credal isms that declare
'Here's what I think, maintain, or feel'—
The core beliefs that people live and swear
By, such as those that simply pair
Off one-to-one and pretty much dictate
What kind of punter's two-horse deal
We voters fall for, courtesy the state.

No end of them, those binaries that set
Thought's limits: liberalism v
The various right-wing isms that would get
Those liberals in a tizz; the debt
That atheists owe to theists; or the need
Of all non-rightists to decree
'Fascist' or 'capitalist' their counter-creed.

For so they go, those couples in their dance
Of contraries, yet not, like strains
Of some disease, a quirk of circumstance,
A viral hop-up, or a chance
Germ-laden kiss—rather, they're what we make
In life-choice terms of what our brains
Lay out as future courses life may take.

The other isms also cover quite
A range, from mild to lethal, but
With this big difference: ailments don't unite,

Divide, or mobilise for right
And wrong like action-plans that call for thought
As well as feeling—not some gut-
Reaction or unthinking stock retort!

A nasty lot, those other kinds of ism,
From rheumatism and a host
Of suchlike ills to—here the dualism
Begins to oscillate—sexism,
Racism, or the whole contested zone
Where some say patho-memes are most
At fault while others chide: 'they should have known!'.

And then *Conservatism*: where to place
That hybrid mode, that curious mix
Of willing, thinking, and the kind of case
That bids pathologists leave space
For diagnoses more inclined to blame
It on some bug that's learned to fix
On feeble brains like hunters on their game.

For who'll deny it's more like a disease,
A plague, a creeping scourge, the way
It spreads and how the symptoms—sneeze or sleaze—
Bring a whole nation to its knees
While the head honchos trouser all they can
By schemes to make the virus pay
For them and all their power-corrupted clan.

Yet let's not push the argument too far
And let them off the hook, those spawn
Of an old breed whose dark, ill-omened star
Sheds light enough to show they are,
And always were, infected to the bone
With all the guile and greed they're born
To learn, then add new vices of their own.

That's why it's this, of all the isms now
Doing the rounds, that lets us gauge
Where moral medicine runs out and how
Some deep infections won't allow
The body politic to see it through
Without, at such a far-gone stage,
What only drastic surgery can do.

One thing's for sure: no germ so lethal, no
Pandemic so deep-reaching, nor
Affliction of that fragile body so
Malignant as the horror-show
Thrust on us by an ism which, in both
Its forms, needs cutting from the core
Of social being like a cancerous growth

Now-Time: a verse-letter to Jeremy Corbyn

To articulate the past historically does not mean to recognize it 'the way it really was' (Ranke). It means to seize hold of a memory as it flashes up at a moment of danger. Historical materialism wishes to retain that image of the past which unexpectedly appears to man singled out by history at a moment of danger.

—Walter Benjamin, 'Theses on the Philosophy of History'

You've sat them out, these past few years,
With all the Tory libels, smears,
And old friends breaking new frontiers
In how to do
The dirt on anyone who steers
A course that's true.

Such lies they told, the tabloid crew,
Such stuff they tried to pin on you,
But you sat tight and saw it through,
Even the jeers
Of Starmerites who staged their coup
To Tory cheers.

They said you'd screwed things good and proper,
Blamed you when Labour came a cropper,
Then put around that crowning whopper
That made you out
An anti-Semite – the show-stopper
They loved to tout.

But now we've seen whose show's the one
That's slated for a dead-end run
To curtain-time, the course begun
Fourteen years back
And primed to self-destruct when done—
Now well on track!

Who'll say, post-Johnson, Truss, Sunak,
'No Corbyn-talk, no change of tack,
Else we'll have City bankers stack
The odds and shun
All Labour's efforts to re-pack
Key points hard-won'.

Just think: if that full-scale campaign
Of slander hadn't let them gain
Another term then who'd complain
Apart from those
With lavish lifestyles to maintain
And ranks to close?

OK, Day One in power—who knows
What you'd have faced from all your foes
In wait out there, the capital flows,
The tabloid bane,
The IMF, and all that goes
To crash the train.

Still you'd an economic brain,
McDonnell, well up to the strain
Of holding out on rough terrain
Where conscience grows
In strength to tell that lot 'refrain!',
Not hold its nose.

They'll get in soon, by hook or crook,
And do it by the Starmer book
Which says: 'now comrades, take a look
At what Blair said
They'd do once in, then what it took
To keep ahead.

Stick to our principles? We're dead!
Think Milibands, David and Ed,
Then ask: why keep the red flag red
If that's what shook
Those floating voters and so led
To No-Win Nook'.

But now we've seen what happens when
The Tories let their natural yen
For tax-breaks put the money-men
In charge of things
And show the nation yet again
Who pulls the strings.

How often it's those final flings,
Those crazy fifth-act happenings,
By which at last high finance springs
The dragon's den
Of corporate greed and shows what brings
Us PowerGen.

Now we've those two oddballs to thank,
Truss and Kwarteng, who broke the bank
(Or would have) and so nearly sank
The ship of state
That City gents said: 'Let's be frank:
Our coup can wait'.

So Truss came on to indicate
Just how far past its use-by date
Their doctrine was: 'why not create
A walk-the-plank
Regime as market laws dictate
Via our think-tank?'.

Let's not pretend we're all on board
For paradise or can afford
To think 'another mouse that roared,
That far-right clique
Of crooks and loons—now best ignored,
Their crackpot streak!'.

No, they'll be there while rich folk seek
To screw the poor through trough-and-peak
Finance that furnishes some freak
Share-hike to hoard:
Wealth for the mighty while the weak
Are fleeced and floored.

But here's the hope: no past event
That once brought hope restored or lent
Old dreams new life was such as went
For nothing, or
Whose putting-down quite simply meant:
Full-time, fixed score.

For if there's one thing spooks the lore
Of banker-dom and gives the poor
Their share of history to shore
Against the bent
Of victor's justice it's the store
Of lives once spent

In struggles that may orient
Our own and thereby represent
The constant need to reinvent
A past that bore,
Till now, no dateline to accent
Save Thermidor.

Long-term or short, that latent past
Has still the wherewithal to cast
A retroactive spell and blast—
Thus Benjamin—
A space for hopes redeemed at last
To enter in.

Then the sign-reader may begin
To turn it back, the victors' spin
On every myth of origin
That might hold fast,
As that old tale of primal sin
Held folk aghast.

Rub history against the grain
Of suchlike tales and their refrain
Will fall on ears that catch a strain
Too long suppressed
By myth-upholders who explain
That they know best.

The Spartacus revolt was first
Of those events that showed the thirst
For freedom, the desire that burst
Forth in the days
When Paris Communards well versed
In rebel ways

Set all good citizens ablaze
With freshly kindled hopes to raise
Their flag of liberty that pays
The tribute nursed
By Spartacists in every phase
Of power reversed.

Think, too, how redolent the name
Of Corbyn now to those who came
Of age back then before the game
Turned nasty and
Some lifelong comrades, to their shame,
Broke faith. They planned

His swift removal lest the stand
He took on arms sales might just land
Them with some hefty reprimand
Or have his aim
Get Labour called a toxic brand—
The war-lords' claim!

Yet it's a name to conjure not
Old feuds, betrayals, on-the-spot
Expulsions or displays of what
The tabloids hailed
As daily rounds of 'Out-the-Trot'
Or 'Corbyn Nailed',

Nor (spare us this!) 'The God that Failed'—
Allende's fame would then have paled
Along with Paris workers gaoled,
Cut down or shot,
And their oppressors' legends trailed
In the prime slot.

Think rather how things stand when we're
Soon, post-election, in the clear
To fix our battered boat and steer
Through choppy seas,
No doubt, but seas that may run near
Some long-sought quays.

Think: NHS in hands at ease
With freely offered expertise,
Not private practices that please
The profiteer
By making rebuilt hips and knees
Now cost us dear.

Think: all schools in the public sphere,
With 'public' meaning not the tier
Of rich kids coddled peer-to-peer
With sky-high fees
To kick Joe Soap out on his ear
('Poor chap, hard cheese!')

But rather schools where good trustees
Ensure no catchment-areas seize
The outsize grants and where the keys
To life, career,
And health don't herald a reprise
Of yesteryear.

Think: 'levelling-up' might then acquire
The sense 'give workers worth their hire
The same life-chances those high-flyer
Execs all had,
Now marked for urban slum, not shire,
Nor Dad to lad.

Think: if the boss now armour-clad
Against the charge of breaking bad
By Tory laws was told to add
New workers, fire
Dud managers, and count it mad
To play the squire.

Then think: those hopes you thought star-crossed
When Corbyn's exit showed the cost
Of Labour treachery weren't lost
For good and all
But shelters from a season's frost
Or sudden squall.

Of course there's lessons yet to learn
And warning-bridges not to burn,
Like Labour ministers who turn,
Once home and dry,
To bad old ways and cease to spurn—
Though with a sigh—

Whatever strategies the guy
Before them (Tory, by the bye)
Saw fit to use and justify
By saying they'd earn
The people's trust, keep ratings high,
Ease press-concern.

'Parliamentary socialism'—that
Odd phrase Ralph Miliband squinted at
Let hopers get the phrase off pat
As history piled
The odds so high that, in to bat
When fortune smiled,

Few leftists would have been so wild
As to foresee them reconciled,
The conjoined terms whose use he filed
As sanguine chat
Amongst those easily beguiled
Then let down flat.

We have it now, the chance to cure
Left melancholy and ensure
The verdict turns out premature,
Though justly brought
By folk who'd had much to endure
In failure's court.

Still, let their witness not cut short
The hopers minded to retort
'So it once seemed, but now the thought
Seems more a lure
To those who'd wish half-truths be taught
Since why abjure

The counter-witness who'd report
The signal episodes that caught
A breath of life blown clean athwart
The embouchure
Of instruments tuned to abort
Hope's overture?

Those bastards had it all their way,
Hung on for ever and a day,
Till the time came for us to say
They'd finally blown
What small reserves they had to pay
For chances thrown.

One thing's for sure: that we'll atone
For sins more weighty if we've grown
So like them that we now disown
Or underplay
The core beliefs we made our own
As rock and stay

Of lifetimes spent beneath the sway
Of capital and so betray

Most grievously the prospect they
Had to postpone
Till its attack-dogs, held at bay,
Let drop their bone.

That's where we are, location known,
Prospectors in a forward zone
Where antecedent hopes once flown
Come to relay
Their message: know you're not alone,
Go as it may'.

It's life or death, and no mistake:
Act now for everybody's sake
Or else Sunak and Co. will make
Those thirteen years
The tremor-time before the quake
When our worst fears

Came true with daily news to shake
Even the hacks ('Give us a break!')
With scenes of squalor such as Blake
Found fit for tears
And had his angels show their stake,
Throw down their spears.

Notes on the author and artist

Chris Norris is Emeritus Professor of Philosophy at Cardiff University where he taught English Literature and then Philosophy until retiring four years ago. He has written many books about philosophy, politics, literary theory, music, and the history of ideas, as well as fourteen previous volumes of poetry, among them *The Trouble with Monsters: poems for dark times* (2018) and *The Folded Lie* (2019; both Culture Matters). He has sung with Cor Cochion Caerdydd (the Cardiff Reds Choir) for more than thirty years and has been active in many socialist, anti-racist, and anti-war movements. He lives in Swansea with his wife Valerie.

Martin Gollan studied sculpture at Edinburgh College of Art in the early 1980s where his early political activism, mainly consisting of boisterous marches and sit-ins, was in response to the Thatcherite policies of the day. Following a motley collection of jobs and a move to the North East of England in the 1990s he has worked mainly in the voluntary sector. He has a studio in Newcastle where he focuses increasingly on painting, printmaking and illustration, is member of the Labour Party, Artists' Union England and is active within grassroots cultural movements. He is married to Sharon and lives in Chester le Street, Co. Durham.

BV - #0076 - 260224 - C3 - 210/148/5 - PB - 9781912710645 - Gloss Lamination